The Cosmos of the Soul

A Spiritual Biography

Michele Doucette

The Cosmos of the Soul: A Spiritual Biography

ISBN 978-1-935786-21-4

Printed in the United States of America by

St. Clair Publications

PO Box 726

McMinnville, TN 37111-0726

http://stan.stclair.net

Table of Contents

Acknowledgements

As a writer, it is of the utmost importance to write about what you know, what you feel, what you believe. In keeping, I have always attempted to write on topics that I feel deeply passionate about.

Throughout the writing of this book, I was continuously encouraged by my husband's unwavering belief in my ability to put words to paper. I trust that my children, Alyssa and Niall, will also be proud of this written effort.

There have been moments, throughout the course of this writing, when I know naught where the words have come. It is my belief that the soul of this cosmos has continued to guide the writing direction and purpose of this publication, and for that I am eternally grateful.

Foreword

The title for this particular tome simply came to be when the words presented themselves. Upon further reflection and deliberation, I began to play with their order, moving back and forth from *The Soul of the Cosmos* to *The Cosmos of the Soul*. It was in attempting to philosophize a plausible and understandable difference between the two that it hit me, a full frontal assault if you will.

I am able to relate to *The Soul of the Cosmos* as being the life force by which we were created. Calling it what you will (God, Goddess, Creator, the Great Spirit, the One, Universal Consciousness, Milord and Milady of the Cosmos, the Great Parent in the Sky, the Manifestor, Infinite Consciousness, All That Is), this life force is the very soul of the entire cosmos of which we are comparable to a fine grain of sand. Even so, we are a most important continuation of the God continuum.

By comparison, *The Cosmos of the Soul* simply brings to mind the universality of all souls, that we are all One; that, in essence, we are all the same. In addition, what is the cosmos of the soul if not an individual journey? How could it be otherwise?

What follows herein, is the story of my own *soul journey*, a sort of spiritual biography, if you will.

I trust that my words will serve to resonate with those that take the time to read.

Namaste.

The Beginning

As a student, I was always taught that writers hold with three essential components in keeping with the creation of any story – beginning, middle and end – and so shall this work flow thusly.

I was born shortly after 6:00 PM on a Monday evening. The date was August 13, 1962. In keeping with the astrological influences of my birth, I am a Leo.

Born six weeks early, weighing in at 3 pounds 5 ¾ ounces, before dropping down to 2 pounds 14 ounces, I had to have possessed the strength and determination of a lion to pull through.

A most terrifying experience for a first time mother, a total of 51 days were to pass before my parents were able to take me home. My father, able to hold me in one hand, lovingly referred to me as his little rat. Now, what do you think of that as a term of endearment?

I was a child that preferred to be alone with my books; not surprising, since I went to school already knowing how to read. My favorite place in the entire school was, of course, the Library.

Being a phenomenal speller, I have always loved to play with the written word. In journeying to the country to visit my maternal grandparents, I took great delight in taking book, paper and pen with me on my independent walks through fields and forest trails. My imagination was quick to soar on those sojourns.

Feeling like the proverbial black sheep of the family, I knew that I was distinctly different from everyone around me. I am sure that this is why I preferred my own company.

It was more than just knowing that I was different, it was also *feeling* that I was different. While I did not embrace my uniqueness, as a young child, I did feel freer to be myself when I spent time in the country.

As a child, I also enjoyed attending Mass.

I can still remember walking up the aisle to kneel and receive the Eucharist for the first time. Mesmerized by the rituals, smells (incense and candles), stained glass windows and statues, as a young lady in Grade 9, I was strongly gravitating towards a life career choice as a Nun within the RC faith.

I always felt as if there were many that did not enjoy reciting the rosary. For me, this was a most profound experience, in that I was able to feel the words with a sense of depth, love and compassion.

An avid reader and researcher by nature, I found myself gravitating toward history courses in school. I am still able to recall Mr. Wilson, a teacher that I had in Grade 10. He had a way of making history come alive, which is why I am now so enthralled with genealogical pursuits as well.

In fact, Mr. Wilson was so inspirational to me that I was soon envisioning a life career related to both history and archaeology, setting out to do just that in September 1980.

Not long thereafter, an unexpected hospital visit, one that introduced me to my niece, Jessica Lynn, born with Trisomy 13 (also known as Patau's syndrome) in November 1982, validated a rather abrupt change in the career path [1] that I had initially been envisioning for myself.

While most Trisomy 13 embryos do not survive gestation and are spontaneously aborted, it was not so for Jessica. Born six weeks early, my oneness moments with her, moments that seemed to stand still, at the Grace Maternity Hospital in Halifax, served to steer me in a totally unexpected career direction – that of Special Education.

It was also in having made this immediate career change at Mount Saint Vincent University, going from being a Bachelor of Arts student (History Major) to a Bachelor of Child Study student, that I met my future husband.

There are times when I feel that Jessica had a hand in this, as well.

---

[1] http://www.portalsofspirit.com/MyCalling.htm

Marrying in August 1985, we immediately departed for the shores of Newfoundland.

I was about twenty-eight years old when my spiritual awakening began. My daughter, Alyssa, was two years old at the time.

Well before Alyssa was born in November 1988, I had stopped going to Mass. It was June 1989 before I had her baptized, out of fear and guilt over what my mother would say if I did not follow suit in the Catholic tradition. Upon Niall's birth in November 1994, I knew that I would be breaking with tradition.

My Gnostic journey had begun.

The Middle

I find it very amusing that what I have deemed to be the middle of this text should also equate to my being what many refer to as middle aged; hence, the middle is where I currently find myself, both literally, as well as figuratively.

All beings, at some point, embark on a spiritual journey. Such is the natural progression of what it means to be human.

When an individual begins seeking answers to questions of considerable importance such as …

Who am I? Why am I here? What is my purpose?

… you can rest assured that he or she is resonating with soul knowingness, cognizant of the fact that the journey towards liberation and destination has begun, for it is this very questioning that drives one forward towards awakening.

Quite simply, you become a seeker of your own truth, the truth that already exists within.

Life shares with us many synchronicities and signs if we are but willing to pay attention. Being the avid reader that I have already shared myself as being, it should not come as any surprise to learn that it took a book to propel me forward, challenging and expanding my limited horizons.

Written by Julia Ingram and G.W. Hardin, The Messengers: A True Story of Angelic Presence and the Return to the Age of Miracles was the book that changed my life; a true story, this book introduced me to Nick Bunick, a prominent and successful Portland, Oregon, businessman.

Never considering himself to be particularly religious, he knew that he had experienced something extraordinary in a past life.

As illuminated in The Messengers, his story began 2,000 years ago when he lived as Paul the Apostle.

Noted as being one of the most extraordinary chronicles of the 20th century, this is a book that details the transformative power of past life regression.

Julia Ingram is a Master Past Life Regression Therapist who additionally specializes in the resolution of spiritual problems, personal and spiritual growth, clarification of one's life path (destiny) and hypnosis.

It was courtesy of this book, The Messengers, that several things occurred, all courtesy of the Internet.

I was able to locate an online forum where 444 experiences were paramount, meeting many wonderful people, many of whom I am still in email contact with today.

I then subscribed to a newsletter, coordinated by Nick. I consider myself blessed to have become online friends with the man whose past life has affected me so deeply.

Thereafter, I was able to locate a copy of In God's Truth, a book written by Nick.

This was *the* book that allowed me, over time, to release myself from fear and guilt, the mechanisms by which the RC Church serves to control the multitude (based solely on my individual experience, of course).

While I had ceased going to church many years prior, I was still being controlled, courtesy of the commanding and dictating voices inside my head.

How comforting it has been to read of these same words in Eckhart Tolle's book, The New Earth: Awakening To Your Life's Purpose, a 2005 publication.

It was in learning about Nick that I was led to read other books and to explore countless websites, all of which served to assist me in challenging the beliefs that were the result of my upbringing.

Interestingly enough, as I slowly began to change on the inside, such was also reflected on the outside, bringing new people (as well as circumstances and situations) into my life.

Knowing that I wanted to be able to assist others in their spiritual quest, my website, Portals of Spirit, [2] was launched in June 2000, midway through the new millennium.

---

[2] http://www.portalsofspirit.com

As alluded to earlier, I'd always felt like I was out of place, that I did not belong, that I was not from this planet. Likewise, I'd always believed the vastness of the Universe to encompass numerous life forms on other planets, in other galaxies.

I felt so much more at home looking up at the stars and spending time, by myself, in nature, compared to spending time with other people. These days, mind you, the climate of the Northern Hemisphere has a tendency to keep me inside more than I would care to admit.

Could we possibly be so narrow-minded as to think that we were the *only* life forms? I am sure that we all have our own stellar heritage [3] stories to share.

Perhaps this is what directed me toward crystals of all sorts, shapes and sizes, especially Moldavite (a meteorite stone that is almost 15 million years old). In keeping, I went on to earn a *Crystal Healing Practitioner* diploma through Stonebridge College in the UK.

---

[3] http://www.lightconnection.org/planetaryorigin/planetaryorigin.html

Evidence that gemstones were used to heal disease can be found in most ancient civilizations. Whether carried in leather pouches, worn as talismans and amulets, compressed into powders or distilled into elixirs, gemstones were known, and used, by natural healers.

In the Vedic tradition, naturopathic medicine was known as Ayurveda, derived from the Sanskrit words *ayur* meaning life and *veda* meaning wisdom.

Ayurveda describes in detail how to prepare elixirs, pastes and powders made from gemstones.

In the first Chinese medical book, written 5,000 years ago by Shen Nung (the Red Emperor), can be found detailed descriptions of gemstones and their influence on the body.

When they come into your possession, crystals can still be holding programs that allow them to work with discordant energies. Deprogramming stops the crystals from working with these energies.

There is a significant difference between programming a crystal as compared to clearing or cleansing a crystal.

Programming imprints a command, thought form or idea, into the internal matrix of the crystal, just as you would put information onto the hard drive of a computer.

Clearing and cleansing merely clears the crystal of the accumulation of unwanted energies.

Despite the fact that the most commonly given method of deprogramming and cleansing one's crystal is to put them in sea salt, I choose specifically *not* to use this method given that salt, also a crystalline structure, is a gatherer of discordant energies (energies that are not in line with the use and purpose of the stone or crystal). In addition, crystals do not like salt because it gets into the microscopic cracks in the faces of the crystal, leeching out their water content. This causes them to dehydrate and start to crack.

I choose, therefore, to clear and cleanse my crystals, before using, with *intent*.

When you draw a symbol, either in your mind or with your hands, or repeat the name of a symbol, you are linking to, and connecting with, the energy of that symbol.

One of the simplest and easiest ways to cleanse, clear and recharge crystals and stones is through the use of one's spiritual energy.

As a *Reiki 2 Practitioner*, I make use of several symbols, first invoking the Choku Rei (for clearing purposes), followed by the Sei Hei Ki (for charging purposes).

There exists a popular trend towards programming a crystal to fulfill a specific purpose, meaning that one attempts to exert their will on the deva (spirit) of the stone. To my way of thinking, this can only be described as a form of imposed slavery upon the free spirit of the crystal.

While there are many who claim programming a crystal is a natural thing to do, I have often wondered whether or not this action might have an adverse effect on the crystal, myself, and/or anyone upon whom the stone might be used; hence, I have never wanted to program any of the crystals that I am guardian to, always choosing to allow the crystal to be themselves.

Although it may seem silly to some, one merely has to stop for a moment to consider if they would wish to be treated in such a manner.

In acting contrary to the rule of *Harm None*, clearly there might well be negative repercussions.

In keeping with the fact that the human body is also of a crystalline nature, the first crystal with which one must work, clean, polish and purify, is naturally, one's self.

Luc Bourgault, author of The American Indian Secrets of Crystal Healing has stated that "it is an illusion to think that you can work effectively with crystals if you have not already started to work on yourself. The crystal is but a tool, for it is not the crystal which will do the work but the person who holds it and who channels their will to heal into it." [4]

I believe, as does Luc, that crystals are living beings, an intimate part of Mother Earth.

---

[4] Bourgault, Luc. (1996). *The American Indian Secrets of Crystal Healing* (pp 17-18). Berkshire, UK: W. Foulsham & Co. Ltd.

In this light, "everything that we think, say and do is registered, expressed and amplified by the crystals. If you possess a power such as that of working with crystals, you have also the responsibility for it. With any power there comes responsibility." [5]

Rough stones (those allowed to remain in their natural condition) are said to possess the greatest healing power and should be placed directly upon the body.

Tumbled stones, more gentle and calming in nature, are best suited for a number of purposes. They can be (a) laid on, or pressed into, the body, (b) used for holding and rubbing, (c) placed directly under one's pillow, and (d) worn over clothing.

Both *precious* and *semi-precious* stones are often crafted into jewelry. An interesting note is that the metals in which these stones are set can also increase the energy levels of the stone itself.

---

[5] Bourgault, Luc. (1996). *The American Indian Secrets of Crystal Healing* (p 24). Berkshire, UK: W. Foulsham & Co. Ltd.

I enjoy placing crystals within my environment to *soak up electro-magnetic pollution* (related to computers, microwave ovens, mobile phones and televisions) and to *bring peace and harmony to an area*.

Crystals have the property of trying to instill order into whatever place they are put, so handling or being surrounded by crystals will always have a beneficial effect. One can also oxygenate the air in any stagnant room by placing crystal clusters about the area.

One of the simplest ways to help balance the entire chakra system is to place a stone of the appropriate color on each corresponding area of the body. It is also a good idea to place a grounding stone between the feet to act as an anchor. By comparison, one may simply visualize color in the area of the chakra while holding specific stones and listening to chakra clearing meditations.

As the chakras open, one gains better health, emotional balance and vitality. In a healthy body, each of these energy vortexes revolves at great speed, permitting vital life energy to flow upward.

When energy is blocked within a specific chakra, symptoms develop in the associated organ or bodily system. The quickest way to regain youth, health and vitality is to assist these energy centers in spinning normally.

Earlier cultures understood water much better than we do today. The ancient Chinese saved water in Jade vases. The Incas and Aztecs saved water in Obsidian jars. African witch doctors used Quartz. Pure water was treasured.

Water can be de-structured, not only by the addition of harmful chemicals, but also by transportation through pressurized pipes, forcing it to move in an artificial way instead of its natural spirals.

As water moves through pipes, it forces the outer electrons to be removed, creating *unstructured* water. This means that all water that we drink or bathe in, that comes from pressurized pipes, has come to be associated with disease.

Water is much more than hydrogen and oxygen. It is the lifeblood of Mother Earth. It is a mysterious, crystalline living entity that nourishes all life.

It is a powerful carrier, mediator and producer of energy. It has the ability to link, transform and carry physical elements and subtle energies. Flower and gem elixirs are a good example of the latter.

Up to 70% of our body is water.

Likewise, 72% of the planet is covered in water.

Hence, healthy, structured water becomes a necessity that cannot be exaggerated.

In my research, I have come across a simple and inexpensive way to safely and effectively structure water.

You will need

[1] 6 quartz crystal points (single crystals) of any size

[2] one double terminated quartz (a point at each end) crystal of any size

[3] a clear glass container (be it a glass or bowl)

[4] the purest water you can find (totally understanding that we can only work with what we have)

[5] a clear intention to restructure and energize the water

You will need to

[1] clean the crystals by holding them under cold running water for a few minutes

[2] fill a plain glass bowl with water

[3] place the double terminated crystal in the middle of the water

[4] arrange the 6 points equally around the container (points facing inward) to form a hexagon

[5] visualize the points charging the DT crystal and the water with vital, healing energy

[6] visualize the DT crystal charging the water with vital, healing energy

While the last two steps are not essential, they do amplify the process.

It is important to leave this arrangement where it will be undisturbed for several hours or overnight.

If you are leaving it outside, be sure to cover the container with a plain glass sheet to prevent contamination. Drink the water every day, making fresh structured water on a daily basis.

You can also avail of an orgone multipurpose disc (coaster style) [6] to orgonize and tachyonize your drinks. Orgone energy is "the fundamental creative life force long known to people in touch with nature, speculated about by natural scientists as the universal ether, employed by acupuncturists, and finally objectified and scientifically demonstrated by the work of the late Wilhelm Reich, M.D." [7]

It was through years of observation and experimentation that Reich was able to identify "many of the basic properties of the orgone energy: it fills all space and is everywhere; it is mass free; it is the primordial, cosmic energy; it penetrates matter; it pulsates and is both observable and measurable; it

---

[6] Nathaniel Pitzer's website located at http://orgonetachyondevices.loveomni.com/oronge%20tachyon%20multi%20purpose%20disc%20.html

[7] http://orgonetachyondevices.loveomni.com/orgone%20information.html

has a strong affinity and attraction to/by water; it is accumulated, naturally, in the organism by food, water, breathing and through the skin." [8]

Reich discovered a way to collect or accumulate orgone energy from the atmosphere, using a combination of organic materials (which serve to absorb and hold the energy) meshed with inorganic materials (which serve to attract and then rapidly repel the energy).

He found that when a person, with their own energy field, "comes into contact with an accumulating device, the two fields make contact and excite each other, creating ... a strong orgonotic charge ... [that] may help strengthen the immune system, improve circulation and raise one's energy levels." [9]

---

[8] http://orgonetachyondevices.loveomni.com/orgone%20information.html

[9] Ibid.

When conducting Reiki treatments, I strap crystals to my wrists (placing them inside athletic bands) with the points facing downwards. Using one on each wrist, of about the same size, will amplify the universal healing energy that flows during the session.

I continue to enjoy meditating within a crystal field (placing crystals around my body). There are many possible lay-outs that can be utilized for a multitude of purposes: balancing and calming, alleviating stress and tension, centering and grounding energies, soothing headaches, easing PMT and menstrual cramps, relieving aches and pains and energizing the body.

As a means of energizing, cleaning and clearing my aura and meridian system, I often lie on my bed, surrounded by 6 to 8 single point crystals, which includes one above my head and another between my feet, points facing inwards for about 10 minutes. This is followed up by a reversal of the crystals, points now facing outwards in order to draw off all unwanted energies, lower high temperatures and draw away any inflammation that may exist.

The final segment of the session involves turning the crystals inward, a final time. In effect, this serves to re-energize and balance the body once more. The total session lasts about 30 minutes.

In summary, it should be clear to the reader, by now, that I feel an affinity with members of the mineral kingdom. In having re-connected in this way, I now feel a sense of grounding to Mother Earth, a sense of belonging that was not there before.

This has been but one aspect of my journey to date.

In further book exploration, the next author to come my way was Doreen Virtue; the book in question being The Lightworker's Way: Awakening Your Spiritual Power to Know and Heal.

This book served to bring me to a *wonderful place* in my life, helping me to better understand that the way we think about ourselves, about others and about life contributes to the way we live.

In the foreword of this book, Louise Hay writes that if we want "to live lives of harmony and well-being, then we must have harmonious, loving thoughts constantly in our mental atmosphere" [10] meaning that we will never "be able to help heal this planet if we criticize and condemn other people, places and events." [11]

This most profound statement is one that we need to take the time to remember. The truth of our being, however, is that we are *already* perfect, whole and complete. Unfortunately, this has been forgotten by a great many.

The beginning of this book delves into Doreen's background as a Christian Scientist. In sharing her experiences, fears, and insecurities, she also discusses, quite frankly, how she began changing her own belief system.

---

[10] Virtue, Doreen. (1997). *The Lightworker's Way: Awakening* 3 *Your Spiritual Power To Know And Heal* (pp ix - x). Carlsbad, CA: Hay House, Inc.

[11] Ibid.

Knowing that she had become empowered to make pertinent changes in her life, I felt that she was enabling, and encouraging, me to do the same.

In the second segment, Doreen shares many different healing modalities and exercises, such as working through one's own issues, clearing one's energy (chakras) and centering one's self.

She also stresses the importance of being aware that one's ego can get in the way of all metaphysical work, as a lightworker or healer, further offering suggestions on how to overcome the voice of the ego.

The next two books, both written by James Twyman, also known as the Peace Troubador, were monumental to my journey; namely, Emissary of Light: A Vision of Peace and The Secret of the Beloved Disciple.

James was called to learn about peace as expressed through Divine Light, an extension of energy that is the very foundation of all life.

He was also called to learn about a physical place belonging to the Emissaries of Light, so that he could reveal their secrets to the world.

In accordance with the belief of the Emissaries, it is necessary that humanity learns how to create a Kingdom of Peace so that we are able to live in a world based solely on love; a world where fear does not exist.

To be successful, we must learn to make a *choice* of peace. By inspiring peace, we are able to give hope. This, then, leads to the desire for forgiveness.

Humanity, it seems, "has chosen its own isolation, imposed its own exile" [12] because we have believed ourselves to be separate and alone. This is merely an illusion, never the reality. It is imperative that people learn to release the fear that is "blocking their extension of love." [13]

---

[12] Twyman, James. (1996). *Emissary of Light: A Vision of Peace* (p 94). New York, NY: Warner Books.
[13] Ibid, p 114.

Once having done so, they can then use that same "energy to transform themselves." [14] It is time for each person to come to "realize how holy they are." [15] The awakening has begun.

This book quickly became my stepping stone to fine tuning this realization into my reality.

If I thought that I was blown away by the messages contained within Emissary of Light: A Vision of Peace, I could not have been more wrong. I was even less prepared for the profound wisdom contained within the very pages of The Secret of the Beloved Disciple, a book so powerfully written that the words will touch the deepest recesses of your heart and soul.

This is a book about miracles that will "transcend the physical world and bring us a step closer to the Divine." [16]

---

[14] Twyman, James. (1996). *Emissary of Light: A Vision of Peace* (p 114). New York, NY: Warner Books.
[15] Ibid, p 116.
[16] Twyman, James. (2000) *The Secret of the Beloved Disciple* (p 9). Tallahassee, FL: Findhorn Press.

In journeying alongside James, you will learn that all we need is love. If we are to obtain this love, we must realize that peace is the key. It is equally important to understand that the law of unity is our reality. By the very nature of the holy individuals that we are, we have always been united with God and with each other.

This book will assist you in changing both your thoughts and perceptions of this current world that we share. It is in becoming love, peace and freedom that we shall begin to experience all.

Nothing is beyond our control. However, you must be prepared to face the biggest challenge of all: the total realization and acceptance of the message contained within this very tome.

Many Lives, Many Masters was my introduction to author Dr. Brian Weiss. A prominent and most traditional psychotherapist, no one was more skeptical than Dr. Weiss when one of his patients began recalling past-life traumas that seemed to hold the key to her recurring nightmares and anxiety attacks.

All of this skepticism vanished when she began to channel personal messages from his deceased father and first-born son. After the revealing of numerous truths, truths that Catherine had never been privy to, Dr. Weiss came to realize that he was never going to be the same. The course of his life was forever changed.

Catherine was also able to reveal ancient truths as channeled through the Master Spirits about such things as past lives, reincarnation, karma and karmic debt, astral planes, different dimensions, vibrations and intuitive powers.

Having read this book, you, too, will find that your life focus becomes more humanistic and less accumulative in nature. This being the case, you shall be on your way to discovering that "happiness comes from filling one's heart with love, from faith and hope, from preaching charity and dispensing kindness." [17] To merely give lip service benefits no one, least of all ourselves. These are the lessons we are all here to learn.

---

[17] Weiss, Brian. (1988) *Many Lives, Many Masters* (p 210). New York, NY: Simon & Schuster Inc.

The next book by Doreen Virtue to grace my path was Divine Guidance: How To Have a Dialogue with God and Your Guardian Angels. With the foreword being written by Nick Bunick, I was, once again, transported back to the subject of The Messengers.

First off, this book is for persons of every faith imaginable. As we are all created and guided by God, we are all sparks of the Divine. This book is a means of teaching us how we can strengthen our spiritual connections.

Doreen will help you understand and recognize true Divine Guidance. It is of prime importance that we learn to become more cognizant of the presence of the Divine within our hearts, minds and bodies.

Many of us experiencc frustration as we struggle to hear that Godly voice that resides within. The more we struggle, the more we end up blocking our spiritual connection links to God. Most are familiar with the phrase *Let Go and Let God*. In essence, this is *exactly* what needs to be done: we must learn to relax.

When we are "willing to consult Divine Guidance about everything, we are freed to let go and enjoy living. We leave the driving to God, and the relaxing knowledge that He provides all of our needs, answers, and desires through this process." [18]

As you delve further into this book, you will learn about the true you and the false you. You will also come to understand the four forms that Divine Guidance takes: (1) visions, images and mental pictures (*Clairvoyance*), (2) sounds, voices and words (*Clairaudience*), (3) feelings and hunches (*Clairsentience*) and (4) thoughts, ideas and inner certainty (*Claircognizance*).

As Nick Bunick writes in the foreword, "Doreen Virtue is truly a bridge into the spiritual world. In Divine Guidance she offers you the key to open the gate and cross the bridge to the other side." [19]

---

[18] Virtue, Doreen. (1998) *Divine Guidance: How To Have a Dialogue with God and Your Guardian Angels* (p 32). Los Angeles, CA: Renaissance Books.

[19] Ibid, p xv.

Creative Visualization was my first introduction to author Shakti Gawain. This is an author who has become an all-time favorite.

Simply put, creative visualization is the art of using mental imagery and affirmations to produce positive changes in your life. By focusing on an idea, feeling or mental image on a *regular* basis, you are giving it positive energy. In keeping with the natural principles that govern the workings of our universe, this positive energy takes on form. In essence, you actually achieve what you have been imagining.

The overall goal is to learn how to use your natural and creative imagination in a more conscious manner. In so doing, you are privy to a technique that will allow you to create what you *truly* want, be it on a physical, emotional, mental or spiritual level.

The method (technique) contained within can help you to change negative habit patterns; improve self-esteem; reach career goals; increase prosperity; develop creativity; increase vitality and improve your health.

In fact, the list is infinitely endless.

If you have a desire to enrich your knowledge and experience, this is the book for you.

If you have a mind that is open enough to try something new while maintaining a positive spirit, this book is for you.

If you have a desire to produce positive changes in your life, this book is for you.

Next came The Path of Transformation: How Healing Ourselves Can Change The World, also by Shakti Gawain.

I was absolutely riveted to this book.

What thoughts, feelings, fears and visions arise when reflecting upon your personal future?

What thoughts, feelings, fears and visions arise when reflecting upon the future of our planet?

These are the very issues explored within this tome.

When one commits to personal growth and change, one has the power to transform their own life.

As "we grow, evolve and expand our consciousness, individually and collectively, the old forms we have created no longer fit." [20]

Ain't that the truth! Real change takes time.

This means that we must have patience and compassion for ourselves and others.

Most people who select this book have already come to the realization that the time for transformation, within their own personal lives, is now; likewise for this remarkable world in which we live.

Questions, however, begin to arise. "How can we support and contribute to that process? How can we do our part, as individuals, to make sure it's going in a positive direction? How do we create real change in our personal lives and in the world?" [21]

---

[20] Gawain, Shakti. (2000). *The Path of Transformation: How Healing Ourselves Can Change The World* (p 15). Novato, CA: Nataraj Publishing, a division of New World Library.
[21] Ibid, p 21.

The answer is, in fact, a very simple and uncomplicated one. By becoming more conscious on an individual level, one is able to bring about the positive change(s) that are needed. "Our lives become more balanced, more fulfilling, and more in alignment with our soul's purpose." [22]

Much like a pebble that is dropped into the stillness of the pond, "the shifts of consciousness we make in our personal lives send out small, but important, waves that ripple through the whole world." [23]

As we grow in our own personal awareness, the mass consciousness also begins to shift accordingly. Each and every one of us plays an integral part in creating our own reality. In essence, we can create the kind of world that we *wish* to experience. We have the ability to co-create with God. This means, then, that we must take full responsibility for our own life experiences.

---

[22] Gawain, Shakti. (2000). *The Path of Transformation: How Healing Ourselves Can Change The World* (p 22). Novato, CA: Nataraj Publishing, a division of New World Library.
[23] Ibid.

Upon recognizing "that the differences and imbalances in our lives are reflections of our own unconscious patterns," [24] we come to the complete understanding that by becoming more conscious of our thoughts, feelings and actions, we have a most powerful tool to affect the changes that are both needed and necessary.

In creating our own reality, we also participate in creating the world reality.

Whatever "attitudes or beliefs are held most deeply and powerfully in the mass consciousness will, for better or worse, be manifested in the collective reality of the world. Unresolved conflict and pain, held in the consciousness of millions of people the world over can ... get reflected back to us in war, in violence in our cities, and in our collective disregard for the rights of other human beings and the well-being of the Earth." [25]

---

[24] Gawain, Shakti. (2000). *The Path of Transformation: How Healing Ourselves Can Change The World* (p 25). Novato, CA: Nataraj Publishing, a division of New World Library.
[25] Ibid, p 31.

We have a role to play in bringing about a positive change in the mass consciousness reality; a role that begins within the very soul of each of us. "It takes a relatively small number of souls moving into alignment with universal faces to have a great impact on our global reality." [26]

Through the individual efforts of each of us, we can *truly* affect significant change. This book will guide you in learning to take action toward conscious growth.

Gregg Braden entered the picture next with The Isaiah Effect: Decoding The Lost Science of Prayer and Prophecy.

A former earth science expert, Gregg now acts as a veteran guide to sacred sites around the world. The Isaiah Effect is an incredibly insightful, and powerfully written, book that combines quantum physics research with the works of the prophet Isaiah and the ancient Essenes.

---

[26] Gawain, Shakti. (2000). *The Path of Transformation: How Healing Ourselves Can Change The World* (p 31). Novato, CA: Nataraj Publishing, a division of New World Library.

Gregg demonstrates how earlier prophecies predicting global catastrophe and suffering may only represent future possibilities, while showing us that we have the power to influence those possibilities.

Seventeen hundred years ago, key elements of our ancient heritage were lost, relegated to the esoteric traditions of mystery schools and sacred orders.

Among the most empowering of these forgotten elements are references to a science with the power to bring everlasting healing to our bodies while also initiating an unprecedented era of peace and cooperation between governments and nations.

We are currently in the process of creating a future for ourselves, a future that even the ancient seers could not predict.

The time for peace, love, compassion and healing has come. Through the reading of The Isaiah Effect, you will come to understand that *your* role is a most necessary and significant one.

This quickly took me through *all* of his other titles; namely, [1] Awakening to Zero Point: The Collective Initiation, [2] Walking Between the Worlds: The Science of Compassion, [3] The God Code: The Secret of Our Past, the Promise of Our Future, [4] The Divine Matrix: Bridging Time Space, Miracles and Belief, [5] An Ancient Magical Prayer: Insights from the Dead Sea Scrolls (cassette), [6] Secrets of the Lost Mode of Prayer: The Hidden Power of Beauty, Blessings, Wisdom and Hurt, [7] Unleashing the Power of the God Code: The Mystery and Meaning of the Message in our Cells (audio CD), [8] The Divine Name: Sounds of the God Code (audio CD), [9] Speaking the Lost Language of God (audio CD) and [10] Awakening the Power of a Modern God (audio CD).

Seldom have I felt the need to seek out an author to such an extent as I have with Gregg Braden.

In addition, he also co-authored a book with James Twyman called Praying Peace: In Conversation with Gregg Braden and Doreen Virtue.

What we focus our mind on grows.

The ancient mystics have always known, for thousands of years, that everything is energy, a fact which has now been scientifically proven by quantum physicists.

Your thoughts are energy, attracting into your life everything that vibrates in alignment with those thoughts.

Think about what you want, and you attract that into your life.

Think about what you do not want, and you attract that, too.

There are seven pathways to peace that are addressed throughout this volume: [1] you are always praying because thought is prayer, [2] whatever you focus your mind on has to increase, [3] to change the world, you must change your thoughts about the world, [4] if you want to experience peace, you must become peace, [5] peace is always present, although it is sometimes hidden, [6] love is the only force in the universe, and [7] the world is already healed.

The purpose of this book is to see what lies behind this wondrous spirit of ours, thereby re-discovering the real source of creation.

James tells us how he came to understand that prayer is the most powerful force in the universe and how peace is the foundation of reality. When we focus on that reality, allowing our spirit to come into total resonance with that reality, then peace truly does prevail on earth. He also takes the time to explain the difference between *praying for peace* and *praying peace* (as per the title).

Prayer is not something we do, it is something we are.

At the very heart of this ancient prayer technology is the alchemical union of thoughts and emotions to produce the feeling of peace.

Gary Zukav was next on the scene with The Seat of The Soul.

Not sure if I would be able to understand what I felt to be a deeply philosophical tome, I was blown away by the very contents of the book itself.

In fact, I was completely riveted.

It is clear from the reading of this work that we are in a time of deep change. How easily we traverse this road, arriving at our final and ultimate destination, depends upon our ability and willingness to honestly see where we are headed.

Gary talks about personality and soul, stressing that when the two become properly aligned we experience *authentic empowerment*.

This is a power that loves life in all forms; a power that does not judge; a power that sees meaningfulness and purpose in all that life, as part of this Earth school, has to offer.

This book will show you how to overcome the eternal power that generates fear. It will enable you to begin to understand your addictions so that you may attempt to overcome them. It will allow you to become more reverent so that you learn to make conscious life choices for the benefit of all.

The Seat of The Soul is a thought-provoking book that needs to be shared with everyone.

One of my most favorite titles has to be Going Deeper: How To Make Sense of Your Life When Life Makes No Sense by Jean-Claude Koven. Quite frankly, this is one of the best books that I have had the pleasure of reading.

I had been delving into spirituality, new-age, metaphysical material, call it whatever you will, since 1990. Following email correspondence with Francine Milano (to whom I am deeply indebted), Jean-Claude took the time to send me an autographed copy to review, wishing me an enjoyable journey (for wish I thank him), in the reading process.

I am not a believer of coincidence. Instead, I am a believer in synchronicity. Feel free to make of this what you will, but Going Deeper was meant to find its way to me.

As per the list in the initial introduction that represents the Wanderers (advanced souls who came to Earth to assist with the impending shift), this is how I equate ......

[1] are deeply saddened by the way humans treat each other (yes)

[2] suffer from allergies and other sensitivities (yes)

[3] feel somewhat alienated, even from friends and loving family (yes)

[4] love to gaze out at the stars (yes)

[5] find yourself thinking that UFOs and channeling might be true (yes)

[6] are more comfortable with plants and animals than with people (yes)

[7] have a sense that you came here to do something important (yes)

As you can see, I score with all components of this list.

I have been told, by a very gifted individual with psychic abilities, that I am an old soul. Does this somehow relate? All is possible, but in having passed through the Veil of Forgetting, I simply cannot remember.

The information presented within this book will greatly unsettle, disturb and/or trouble those who believe in the illusion; it will also serve to challenge and summon those that do not.

The illusion, quite simply, lies in the perpetuated belief that we are separate from the Creator. Such has been, and continues to be, the primary role of organized religion. Such remains the hook. This is why Going Deeper comes across as incredibly threatening to the greater multitude.

It has been my belief that in order to change the world, I must first begin with myself. It may seem rather simplistic, but Jean-Claude certainly agrees. Using the analogy of the pebble tossed into the pond, as the ripples permeate outward, so, too, does one's energy signature, be it from a peace and love-filled mindset or from a fear-filled mindset. It is clear to me that one's thoughts, words and actions greatly impact the totality of the planet; hence, I have nowhere to begin but with myself.

For those of you who also find yourselves situated outside the fray (as in organized religion), this is the next book you need to purchase.

After reading Going Deeper, you will never look at life in the same light again. Quite simply, be prepared for the ride of your life!

Will it be an easy task? Some days, yes; some days, no.

Am I up to the challenge? I believe that I am.

Am I open to the possibilities that exist? Most definitely.

Quite clearly, this is the book that is sending shock waves through the metaphysical community.

Such a statement entices and beckons one to come forward and explore the possibilities, does it not?

May *you* be the very next individual to do so.

In April 2008, I received a copy of an interview conducted by Allan Silberhartz, host of the Bridging Heaven and Earth website, [27] featuring Jean-Claude.

I am now going to take the time to share some of the noted key points with you. Jean-Claude's words are in bold type.

---

[27] http://www.heaventoearth.com/

When you play the game of discovery and you don't listen to the word of, or the doctrine of, and all that kind of stuff, and you go out there ... every situation you are in, every person that you meet, every flower that you see, every tree ... no matter what it is, is God.

There is nothing in all creation besides God, so for me, God cannot be a noun. There is no such thing as the Creator. God is the unfoldment of creation itself; not that God is *in* all things, but that God *is* all things. There is no separation. This is the illusion.

When you see it from that other vantage point, there is no separation, there is only Oneness. Infinity, beyond anything we could ever grasp is One.

What a powerful opening, wouldn't you say?

Follow your passion, or as Joseph Campbell would say, follow your bliss. If it doesn't resonate inside with the essence of who you are, then keep looking for something else that does.

This is such a truth filled statement.

We are each an aspect of the Oneness, experiencing itself from the point through which we view. So our gift to this vast cosmic hologram is our uniqueness. Not our ability to conform, but our ability to follow, with courage, the curiosity we had as a child, joyously and fearlessly.

I have never heard our gifts put quite this way before, but it works for me!

It is like you are in the middle of this incredibly beautiful running river. You don't have any interest in the sides. You don't want to get entangled in the side currents any more.

It's taking you to some infinite destination, and all you care about is the journey of being in the river. There is no destination. Each moment, then, becomes magical. The trick is when you show up.

When you [as in your consciousness] **are there, if you can be there and evoke it for another being, and the two of you can create a unique space in the Cosmos, that is magic! You fall in love. You literally fall in love with**

every being that you meet, when you show up, and they are willing and trust enough.

All I can say to that is ... wow!

Jean-Claude then goes on to talk about the importance of creating in every moment, bringing joy, purpose and value to everyone that we meet. Such becomes the “game of life,” to use his words.

When we compress ourselves into an illusion and ego, and hold that as value, and then we get together with other little egos, and we think that because we have enough consensus, enough of us believe a particular thing, this must be truth with a capital T.

Unfortunately, such is the “truth” that we are taught.

Inside the inner being that is that exquisite gem, that infinite God continuum that we all are, there is only the One. It is not that you are *part* of the Oneness, you *are* the Oneness.

In all of creation, there is only you, and that is equally true for every being on this planet.

Whereas, by comparison, this is the *real* truth with a capital T.

And when people say what did you learn down here, I say only one thing ... what you see, depends on where you are looking from. If you absolutely have an investment holding onto the point from which you view, it is not a shock to anybody that what you see never changes. If you constantly are willing to shift the point from which you view, you get to realize that you know nothing.

This last statement, in and of itself, is an extremely liberating one, is it not?

In order to understand the illusion of the 'Matrix', you have to have some degree of mastery over it **to be able to understand, with compassion, what others go through and what they are still caught in, and then try to create the bridge between heaven and earth.**

It's the ineffable journey that expands from the instant into the infinite. The music that is played in the crack between the keys, that's what you listen to, but *not* with your ears, but *with* your whole resonate heart, with the heart/mind.

This is something that I can fully relate to as I attempt to more completely tune into my own intuition.

The rest of my life now is devoted to trying to figure out other ways of expressing this, creating the vehicles for others to experience, if even for a small instant, who they really are and what the magnificence of every single being on this planet is. You extend through all of creation ... creation is only you. That is true of every being on the planet. It simply doesn't get any bigger than this.

Quite simply, this is an amazing dedication: assisting others to experience the same, even if only for a small instant.

No matter where you go in the infinite, no matter what direction you move, you meet yourself. And the journey, if you understand creation, that larger creation myth, the purpose behind, the impetus behind, all creation is to *allow the Oneness to experience itself infinitely*.

While this is *not* what we, the multitude, have been taught, it is something that, when ready, will resonate deeply within as the complete and ultimate truth.

All of creation is simply a gradation of awareness, a gradation of consciousness.

What would it be like? What an amazing experiment it would be if we were to create an illusion in which we put points of consciousness, that perceive themselves separate and abandoned by the One, and separate from each other.

Which is actually our current existence in the here and now.

Now view the Oneness as a vast, infinite, cosmic hologram to which we are all connected.

Every experience, every emotion, every word, every thought we ever have, constantly, instantly, in real time, gets fed into that cosmic hologram, which is the All That Is. And now we can begin to understand the richness of the potential of the information that we could send up, if we have fearless courage, if we experience joy, if we actually come and touch with our own passion.

That's real grist for this mill, not the pap of being a good sheep and merely following.

Jean-Claude also talks about carnivals whereby individuals spend an outrageous amount of money to win a cheap prize, thinking they have come away with something worthwhile for their endeavors.

Unfortunately, this is how we go about most of our lives, spending money on things that do not give us joy, that do not enhance our bliss.

The only thing life asks of you, in order to be magnificent, is to show up.

Such equates wholeheartedly with Eckhart Tolle's being present in the now. Unfortunately, we have a tendency to rob ourselves of the moment. It appears that multi-tasking, which is something I have mastered, and applauded myself on, robs us of our presence in the now.

Jean-Claude talks about **the zone**, a place, devoid of ego, that **is being so completely in the moment that the you disappears.** At some point, we have all experienced the zone. I was so totally able to relate to these words because this is exactly how I feel when I am engaged in my writing.

I am a member of the Truth of the Moment club. Just don't hold me to it tomorrow. Whatever this archive said, just remember that it occurred on this particular day, in this particular year. And that is what I thought I saw then. Tomorrow, I think I'll see something else.

To know that we are constantly changing can only be a positive thing.

It is so true when he shares that **each of us carries a load** [meaning that we each carry the load of our own perception] and **the way out of the illusion, is when we help lighten each other's load. If I can help you lighten your load and you can help me lighten mine, such will open this up as a way for all of us serving each other,** which brings to mind the song, *He Ain't Heavy, He's My Brother* by the Hollies, a long time favorite.

When people go into their own personal paths, a lot of them are quite selfish. "I'm trying to become enlightened. When I'm enlightened, then I can help". The trick is to be there now. How about today?

So very true, and yet this is something we are all guilty of, at some point in our lives.

When you work in free will, the only motivating factor is curiosity. What is *this* like? What is *that* like? I *don't* like that, but I *do* like this. Now you are in the heart/mind of God ... my will and thy will and thy will be done. This is your innate pure curiosity finding expression through you in your life.

I so like how he has stated this.

When asked if he had a goal, his response was in the affirmative. He continues by saying that he has three things he shares with people up front.

The *first* one is increased awareness; constantly looking to increase personal consciousness, for yourself and all others.

The *second* one is to rekindle the curiosity that you had as a child, that you bartered in order to fit in. The illusion creates the illusion that you have to sell out in order to survive.

And the *third* one, the most important, is to become self empowered, become self referential, to be able to look outside of yourself.

I would love to be so disappeared, to not fight my ego, not have all those things going on inside of me, that I could serve more purely. I would love it.

Do I think that there are beings on the planet who can do it? Absolutely. I think all have this within us, that innate core of our being. But there is still too much of me in the equation, and so, for me, it is still an ongoing process.

This, too, is where I am, trying my utmost to disentangle from the ego equation.

When you talk about the paradigm shift, I think that this is where we are shifting to ... a level of entanglement and merging that is of the level of intimacy where we are totally in each other's minds. Our minds are merged, so we don't even need to coalesce a thought, to have an expression. When the two become one, that level of communication is far more intimate than bridging.

What an amazing and revolutionary view, one of complete Utopia.

If any of these interview points have intrigued you, please find yourself a copy of Going Deeper: How To Make Sense of Your Life When Life Makes No Sense.

And now for a continuance of God *is* all things.

Hidden Truth: Forbidden Knowledge became my insight into Dr. Steven Greer.

As per Dr. Brian O'Leary, an Apollo Astronaut, "Steven has provided amazing leadership in penetrating the mysteries not only of the phenomenon itself, but the shadowy corners of U.S. government and corporate cover-up of it. As a result, Dr. Greer has proven himself time and time again as a fearless and energetic warrior on the leading edge of planetary change." [28]

Firstly, he founded the Center for the Study of Extraterrestrial Intelligence, also known as CSETI, introducing the concept of ambassadorship between humans and off-planet cultures.

---

[28] Greer, Steven. (2006). *Hidden Truth- Forbidden Knowledge* (p 9). Crozet, VA: Crossing Point, Inc.

Next, he embarked on the difficult task of locating and securing video/DVD testimonies of over 100 U.S. government UFO/ET witnesses under The Disclosure Project.

He is also the founder of Space Energy Access Systems (SEAS), thereby "providing support to inventors with revolutionary new energy technologies that could give the world clean, cheap and decentralized energy, thus ending the oil, coal, and nuclear Age and the virtual end of human-caused pollution and climate change." [29]

We are all one in Spirit. It is in acknowledging and experiencing this unity that you can be one with all of creation, including life on other planets and in other galaxies, for the entire cosmos is our home. "The entirety of creation is sacred and every being is sacred, because spirit, the awake Being, is the very fabric of all that there is." [30]

---

[29] Greer, Steven. (2006). *Hidden Truth- Forbidden Knowledge* (p 9). Crozet, VA: Crossing Point, Inc.

[30] Ibid, p 270.

Further to this, Steven shares that "it is always perfectly one, even if it's playing and displaying upon itself as if it is different. The challenge is to see the oneness within the difference, and also enjoy the difference." [31]

This book has a depth to it that you will not expect. If you wish to better understand how to attain higher states of awareness through meditation, you, too, will be pleased to know that Dr. Greer has created a course in advanced mantra meditation called Cosmic Consciousness. [32]

In keeping with yet another fearless and energetic warrior, Dan Millman, author of Way of the Peaceful Warrior, now enters the picture. This is yet another book that will change your life. In fact, you may not even realize that you have changed until you catch yourself thinking in a different way.

---

[31] Greer, Steven. (2006). *Hidden Truth- Forbidden Knowledge* (p 270). Crozet, VA: Crossing Point, Inc.

[32] http://www.disclosureproject.org/cd-dvd.shtml

The more conscious we are, the easier it is to break free. You just have to wake up to the *real* you, the you that has always been.

To dwell on the past is to rob the future.

To worry about the future is to rob the present.

The reality that exists is to learn to live in the now.

Socrates shows Dan the difference between the brain and the mind. Dan questions the positive uses for the mind and the great minds in history. Socrates responds by showing him that there aren't any great minds, that there are only great brains, saying further that "*Mind* is one of those slippery terms like *love*. The proper definition relates to your level of consciousness." [33]

Socrates continues to explain how the brain has abstract processes of dealing with information, called the intellect,

---

[33] Millman, Dan. (2000). *Way of the Peaceful Warrior* (p 52). Tiburon, CA: HJ Kramer Inc.

adding that "nowhere have I mentioned mind. The brain and mind are not the same. The brain is real; the mind isn't." [34]

He later explains how the mind is all the random uncontrolled thoughts that cloud your brain, thereby equating it to that of a useless tool. This difference between the mind and brain is not something most think about in their regular lives.

In the reading of Dan's words, you will find truth in what Socrates is saying. The hidden message being … do not let your mind get in the way of your brain by thinking useless thoughts (referred to as cerebral fidgeting) as such inhibits the clarity of life in the now.

While I had known about Eckhart Tolle for some time, the book to really hit home for me was <u>The New Earth: Awakening To Your Life's Purpose</u>.

Many readers will, by now, have known that Oprah was responsible for the creation of a New Earth Online Class.[35]

---

[34] Millman, Dan. (2000). *Way of the Peaceful Warrior* (p 52). Tiburon, CA: HJ Kramer Inc.

Eckhart has shared that understanding the book is not necessary, it is only secondary, while the first item of importance is to *experience the truth* of the book. Eckhart also tells us that the essence of the book cannot be understood on a conceptual level. Anyone who finds the book meaningful is *already* awakening and/or awakened.

The basis for your life is the present moment. One must accept, and be grateful for, this moment as it is. If you are not friendly with life, life cannot support you.

One must concern one's self with their own journey, accepting that it is not yet for everyone. You can only know what presence is by being present. The question, according to Eckhart, that needs asking is … what is my relationship with the present moment?

One must become more alert.

One needs to identify if negativity, of any sort, is involved. If this is the case, then one is fighting something. In this instance, one is turning the present moment into an enemy.

---

[35] http://www.oprah.com/oprahsbookclub/A-New-Earth-Syllabus

It is a well know fact that what you resist always persists.

It is imperative, therefore, that one make peace with the moment. This does not mean that you have to approve of the situation, but you must make peace with the situation so as to release yourself from the negativity that seeks only to enslave.

You must accept something before you can work toward changing it.

Action comes out of the acceptance.

The change that comes out of acceptance creates a totally different experience; one empowered by life itself.

Spirituality has *nothing* to do with what you believe and *everything* to do with your state of consciousness.

Spirituality refers to how present you are in the moment.

Are you in your thoughts or are you there as awareness behind your thoughts?

The next crucial question, then, to be asked is … are you present in this moment?

I have attempted to go into depth with the many books that have been *key* in illuminating my path.

I trust that the reader will resonate with some of these titles, wanting to explore them as well.

In summation, I have learned to equate rigid dogma with blind faith. Whilst there was a time when I was a complete believer in this particular approach, such has not existed for me in a very long time.

Now I take the time to read, write, research, examine and challenge, all in order to establish my own inner truth, a truth that exists between two sources: myself and my Creator. There is no other source that I need call upon. I need no longer search outside of myself because my search has since become an inner one.

Learn deeply of the mind and its mystery for therein lies the true secret of immortality is the message put forth in The Secret in the Bible.

This "sixteen-worded sentence was extracted from the ancient *Book of God*, a mysterious old document written on fabric of an unknown nature, and highly regarded by the Ancients thousands of years ago" [36] and is the message that serves to highlight my journey. While I may still enhance my journey with books, music and crystals, I am not in search of a Guru. I have no need of such a person, for I am my own Guru.

The most notable fact in keeping with Eckhart Tolle is that he has allowed me to see, with additional clarity, that my role, my purpose, simply involves my being able to *sense my essential Being-ness, the I AM, in the background of my life at all times and in all situations*.

It is so simple, and yet so ultimately profound. This, then, becomes my own personal ascension.

---

[36] Bushby, Tony (2003). *The Secret in The Bible* (p 6). Queensland, AU: Joshua Books.

The End

I do not foresee the end as being the literal end. In retrospect, what is a perceived ending, if not a new beginning?

The ancient mystics have always known, for thousands of years, that everything is energy, a fact which has now been scientifically proven by quantum physicists.

Your thoughts are energy, attracting into your life everything that vibrates in alignment with your thoughts.

Think about what you want, and you attract that into your life.

Think about what you do not want, and you attract that, too.

According to the teachings of Abraham [37] ......

The Universe is not punishing you or blessing you. The Universe is responding to the vibrational attitude that you are emitting. *The more joyful you are*, *the more Well-Being flows to you*, and you get to choose the details of how it flows.

– Excerpted from a workshop in Phoenix, AZ, on Saturday, February 24, 2001

When you talk about *what* you want and *why* you want it, there's usually less resistance within you than when you talk about *what* you want and *how* you're going to get it. When you pose questions you don't have answers for, like how, where, when, who, it sets up a contradictory vibration that slows everything down.

– Excerpted from a workshop in San Antonio, TX, on Saturday, January 29, 2005

---

[37] http://www.abraham-hicks.com/lawofattractionsource/index.php

It only takes about 30 days to change a habit. Not because you need 30 days. You could do it in 68 seconds if you could hold your vibration there, but you have to consciously make that decision.

– Excerpted from a workshop in Napa, CA, on Sunday, March 2, 1997

As you give thought to your future – your future that may be 10 years; your future that may be 5 years; or your future that is 60 days away – you literally begin pre-paving. And then, as you move into those pre-paved moments, and as that future becomes your present, you fine tune it by saying *This is what I now want*. And all of those thoughts that you have put forth about your future, right down to this moment when you are now intending what action you want to take, will all fit together to bring you precisely that which you now want to live.

– Excerpted from a workshop in “The Law of Attraction, The Basics of the Teachings of Abraham” on Saturday, July 1, 2006

You are all perfect and expanding; you are all adored and worthy; *you are all here having your exposure to experiences and doing the best that you can from where you are*. You have not been sent here in a test or trial; you're here as creators as part of an expanding Universe. You can't have it both ways. You can't have, at the root of that which you are, Well-Being, and then have that same root of Well-Being have the capacity to pronounce you evil. It is vibrationally impossible. That judging vengeful God is manufactured from humans' place of deepest despair.

– Excerpted from a workshop in Fort Collins, CO, on Saturday, June 19, 2004

You cannot focus upon the weaknesses of one another and evoke strengths. You cannot focus upon the things that you think they are doing wrong, and evoke things that will make you feel better. *You've got to beat the drum that makes you feel good when you beat it. And when you do, you'll be a strong signal of influence that will help them to reconnect with who they are.*

– Excerpted from a workshop in Washington, DC, on Saturday, October 16, 2004

You cannot get sick enough to help sick people get better. You cannot get poor enough to help poor people thrive. *It is only in your thriving that you have anything to offer anyone. If you're wanting to be of an advantage to others, be as tapped in, tuned in, turned on as you can possibly be.*

– Excerpted from a workshop in San Diego, CA, on Saturday, February 15, 2003

You have been oriented that you must pay a price in order to get somewhere, and in the process, you've come to believe that getting there must be really important, therefore, it must be your purpose. And we say, but *if you're not getting to joy, then you've gotten nowhere. Joy is really where you're going.*

– Excerpted from a workshop in Boca Raton, FL, on Saturday, December 13, 2003

You are really individual beings, with very special talents, and it would be nice if teachers had the time, or parents had the awareness or skill, to see the children as the very individual, very special beings that they are. So that rather than trying to drum them into one category, they are, instead, appreciating the special insight that each child brings to the sea of diversity and contrast which is the stuff that creation comes from.

– Excerpted from a workshop in Atlanta, GA, on Saturday, September 13, 1997

No matter what it is, *if you really want it, and you get out of the way of it, it will happen.* It must be. It is Law. It can be no other way. It's the way this Universe is established. *If you want it and you relax, it will happen.*

– Excerpted from a workshop in Cincinnati, OH, on Saturday, September 21, 2002

Enlightenment means literally aligning to the Energy of my Source. And genius is only about focusing because the Law of Attraction takes care of everything else. Physical humans often want to make enlightenment about finding some process and moving through the process that has been pre-described. But *true enlightenment is moving to the rhythm of the internal inspiration that is coming in response to the individual desire.* Enlightenment is about allowing my connection to the Source that is me for the fulfillment of the things that I have individually defined here in my time/space reality. That's as good as it gets!

– Excerpted from a workshop in Boulder, CO, on Saturday, June 7, 2003

Abraham is not about guiding anyone toward or away from anything. We want you to make all of your decisions about your desire. You have that right. You should be able to do that. *Our only desire is that you discover the way to achieve your desires*.

– Excerpted from a workshop in Monterey, CA, on Tuesday, March 20, 2001

Appreciation and self-love are the most important tools that you could ever nurture. *Appreciation of others, and the appreciation of yourself is the closest vibrational match to your Source Energy of anything that we've ever witnessed anywhere in the Universe*.

– Excerpted from a workshop in Spokane, WA, on Tuesday, May 30, 2000

Being happy is the cornerstone of all that you are! Nothing is more important than that you feel good! And you have absolute and utter control about that because you can choose the thought that makes you worry or the thought that makes you happy. *You have the choice in every moment*.

– Excerpted from a workshop in Sacramento, CA, on Saturday, March 15, 2003

As you can see, I thoroughly resonate with the teachings of Abraham.

I have also discovered Ho'oponopono, an ancient Hawaiian method of stress reduction (release) and problem solving.

Essentially, Ho'oponopono means "to make right with the ancestors, or to make right with the people with whom you have had relationships." [38]

---

[38] Tad James Companies (2005). *The Huna Process of Ho'oponopono*. Retrieved April 12, 2008 from http://www.ancienthuna.com/ho-oponopono.htm

Quite simply, it is a process of letting go of any toxic energies that may be residing within your physical being so that you can allow a new space for the healing power of your Divine Self.

The key Ho'oponopono words that you recite over and over again are: *I Love You*, *I Am Sorry*, *Please Forgive Me*, *Thank You*.

Knowing that all of your memories are housed in your subconscious, as soon as you say *I Love You*, these very words begin the remediation process.

Feel free to explore the following sites related to Ho'oponopono.

Ho'oponopono Insights (Saul Maraney) [39]

Ho'oponopono For Today Blog [40]

The Easiest Way: Self-Identity Through Ho'oponopono [41]

---

[39] http://hooponoponoinsights.wordpress.com/

[40] http://hooponoponofortoday.blogspot.com/

Ho'oponopono: Making Things Right [42]

Educate Yourself: Ho'oponopono [43]

There is also a new Ho'oponopono Yahoo Group [44] that many might like to explore.

While I have not been completely successful in mastering meditation, I am endeavoring to master what is termed *breathing meditation*, the purpose of which is to calm the mind and develop inner peace. Breathing meditations can be used alone. They can also be used as a preliminary exercise to additional types of meditative practices.

With eyes closed, I focus my complete, and conscious, attention on breathing. Inhaling and exhaling naturally, I try to become aware of the sensation of the breath as it enters and leaves the nostrils. It is this very sensation that is the object of the meditation. All else, save this breath sensation, is ignored.

---

41 http://www.mabelkatz.com/
42 http://www.cancerlynx.com/huna.html
43 http://educate-yourself.org/zsl/hooponopono25jul06.shtml
44 http://groups.yahoo.com/group/ho_oponopono_aloha/

At first, the mind still partakes of cerebral fidgeting. In fact, most people feel that the meditation is making the mind feel even busier. In retrospect, however, you are merely becoming more aware of just how busy the mind actually is.

You will be greatly tempted to follow through with the different thoughts that arise. Keep focusing on the sensation of the breath. If your mind does wander, immediately return to the breath, repeating this, as often as necessary, until the mind settles on the breath.

The benefits to patiently practicing this breathing meditation are such that gradually, as the thoughts subside, you are able to experience a sense of inner peace and relaxation. Your mind will feel lucid and spacious. You will feel refreshed.

As the turbulence of the distracting thoughts subsides, and the mind becomes still, a deep happiness and contentment arises from within.

This feeling of well-being is what helps everyone cope with the stresses and difficulties from everyday life.

It can be said that much of the stress and tension we experience comes from the mind. Many of the problems that we experience, including ill-health, are both caused and aggravated by this stress.

Taking the time to engage in this breathing meditation, 10 to 15 minutes each day, will enable you to reduce this stress. You will feel much calmer and difficult situations will become easier to deal with.

Meditative Breathing [45]

Diaphragmatic Breathing [46]

Online Meditation Breathing [47]

Conscious Breath [48]

Breathing Meditations [49]

---

[45] http://serenityonlinetherapy.com/meditation.htm
[46] http://www.swamij.com/diaphragmatic-breathing.htm
[47] http://www.meditation-techniques.net/breathing-meditations.htm
[48] http://www.meditation-techniques.net/meditations/consciousbreath.htm
[49] http://www.yogateacher.com/text/meditation/on-line/breath.html

Mindfulness of Breathing and Four Elements Meditation [50]

Mindfulness Meditation [51]

Mindfulness Meditation Technique [52]

A Moment of Calm [53]

Knowing that *now* is the time to reclaim your power, how do you actually begin to think anew for yourself?

As already shared in an essay of mine called *Our Current Collective Reality Is Most Shocking Indeed*, David Icke makes note of several steps with which to begin.

"Step One: Refuse to have another tell you what to think and do with your life. What matters is that you are you and not what someone else is telling you to be. Respect the freedom of others to do the same.

---

[50] http://www.buddhanet.net/pdf_file/fourelements.pdf
[51] http://www.4mindfulnessmeditation.com/
[52] http://www.alternativedepressiontherapy.com/mindfulness-meditation-technique.html
[53] http://www.beliefnet.com/Health/1999/12/A-Moment-Of-Calm.aspx

Step Two: As the process of unplugging continues, things that mattered to you before become less important and your outlook on life and others starts to transform. You become more tolerant of yourself and others. Your attitudes to everything change once the recognition of the illusion goes deeper and deeper and you start to *be* that awareness rather than just intellectually accepting its existence. Don't think it, know it. Don't try to do it, just do it. These are very different states of being. When you become more consciously aware of the illusion, you can begin to enjoy it without all the hang-ups that imprison us when we think it is real. We can have fun and express our desires, as long as they don't impinge on the freedom of others.

Step Three: Taking ... responsibility and ceasing to blame others, or ourselves come to that, is to take a massive step on the freedom road. The power the Illuminati use to control and manipulate is only the power we give away to them and others every day. The most destructive expression of this is blaming others for our plight. In truth, only *we* have that power if we choose to use it; but if we believe that others are in control of our destiny, we will create that reality.

Step Four: We need to start focusing on the right to freedom of expression" [54] for all. This can also be translated to treating all persons with respect. If we believe that division and separateness exists, the Matrix has us for it promotes this duality.

Oneness = Love = Balance

Hatred = Illusion of Division = Disharmony

Once you "realize that your programmed reactions are not *you* there will be far more harmony and peace in your life. There are still moments when the program will con you into reacting, but the more you express consciousness, the less this will happen and the quicker you will apply the brake when it does." [55]

---

[54] Icke, David. (2003). *Tales from The Time Loop* (pp 445-448). Wildwood, MO: Bridge of Love Publications USA.

[55] Ibid, p 185.

In addition, "we don't need to learn, we need to *un*learn what the program has manipulated us to believe. Mind is not the road to enlightenment; it is the barrier to it. Knowledge and knowing is not the same thing – one is mind, the other consciousness. We don't need to learn, but to awaken from the hypnotic trance and remember who we are. When we do, we cease to *think* and start to *know*. Some call this intuition or *following the heart*." [56]

What David shares next can be just a tad confusing, but completely relevant to coming back to one's self.

To "truly connect in awareness with the One, we need to stop making choices, stop trying to change anything and have no sense of purpose. To be without purpose does not mean to sit down and do nothing; it is to cease to identify who you are with what you are doing and no longer let what

---

[56] Icke, David. (2003). *Tales from The Time Loop* (p 187). Wildwood, MO: Bridge of Love Publications USA.

you do define you. What you do *just is* instead of what you are." [57]

It gets just a wee bit more integral in this next segment.

If we "don't pursue purpose, choice and change, does that mean we just sit around and do nothing while the Illuminati impose terror, control and mayhem? Well, yes and no. It is not about *doing*, but *being*. To *do* is to make a choice to do. It is a process of thought and that is the program, the Matrix, creating polarities. To *be* is to *know* – the One. The pursuit of purpose and *doing* gets in the way of that. Oneness is the balance of all, and the Illuminati agenda is not balance, but polarities. To challenge the Illuminati is not balance, but polarity. To *be* is to encompass them *both* and identify with *neither*." [58]

---

[57] Icke, David. (2005). *Infinite Love is the Only Truth - Everything Else is Illusion* (pp 191-192). Wildwood, MO: Bridge of Love Publications USA.

[58] Ibid, p 193.

In continuation, "when we come from the perspective of Oneness and move with the flow of knowingness, things just happen without us needing to choose, think, fight or pursue."[59] In essence, therefore, "the road to freedom and Oneness is not to create polarities, but to encompass them."[60]

If, indeed, we want change for the better, "we need to understand first what we have to deal with, and secondly that real change will not come from the top down, but rather from the bottom up"[61] which clearly means that, in order to be in control of our own lives, we must also take responsibility for ourselves.

Collectively, all are responsible for the current state of affairs.

---

[59] Icke, David. (2005). *Infinite Love is the Only Truth - Everything Else is Illusion* (p 193). Wildwood, MO: Bridge of Love Publications USA.

[60] Ibid.

[61] Greaves, Richard. "Who Runs the World?". The Truth Campaign magazine. Autumn 2001: Issue 22, page 26.

For "meaningful changes to take place ... it begins in the hearts and minds of individuals who look around and see things for what they are." [62]

As an individual, I am doing my best to disengage in a manner that befits me at the present time.

[1] Total detachment from the media.

I no longer watch the news on TV. I have stopped reading the newspapers. I do not listen to the news on the radio. I have stopped reading news related magazines. This was the first step for me in releasing myself from the fear and negativity that abounds within the Brotherhood controlled media.

As a result of my Masters of Education in Literacy program, I came to better understand that TV stations report what they are told to report; namely, biased media events which serve to perpetuate the imbalance that exists.

---

[62] Greaves, Richard. "Who Runs the World?". The Truth Campaign magazine. Autumn 2001: Issue 22, page 27.

Once awareness has been heightened to the degree that the viewer can think of nothing else, focusing and channeling their energies on the negative events (these seem to be the only ones portrayed), such continues to perpetuate the divide, rule and conquer mentality which feeds on unstable emotions.

[2] Seeking the truth.

I am learning to detach from what I have been manipulated into believing, because therein lies the containment, the imprisonment. I am challenging and seeking truth in whatever form that resonates within my very soul, within my very consciousness. I am remembering.

[3] Becoming the change I wish to see in the world.

How am I working on this? By letting go of fear, and refusing to give it power; by placing an increased focus on the positive so as to generate more of this vibration; by connecting with my highest level of wisdom; by allowing love and inspiration to guide what I deem most appropriate for myself; by becoming peace; by becoming forgiveness;

by doing unto others as I would have them do unto me; by celebrating diversity; by demonstrating compassion; by meditating and surrendering to the stillness; by listening to my intuitive heart; by being brave enough to transform my very being.

[4] Continuing to focus on the good and the positive.

There are exciting, wonderful and beautiful things happening on the planet, many of which are extremely promising. "On the one hand we have this carcass of an old world that is dying. It is going through the death throes. And yet, here is this new world that has already been born, and is growing and is going to continue for thousands of years. It isn't going to be the end of *the* world: it is the end of *an old world* and the simultaneous establishment of a *new* one. We are already in the early stages of the golden era of the human race." [63]

---

[63] Greer, Steven. (2006). *Hidden Truth - Forbidden Knowledge* (p 226). Crozet, VA: Crossing Point, Inc.

It is so true when Dr. Greer shares that "the entirety of creation is sacred and every being is sacred, because spirit, the awake Being, is the very fabric of all that there is. And it is always perfectly one, even if it's playing and displaying upon itself as if it is different. The challenge is to see the oneness within the difference, and also enjoy the difference." [64]

[5] Following my bliss.

Joseph Campbell, now deceased, is responsible for three profound words; namely, follow your bliss. Many have lived their very lives in keeping with this principle.

As you discover what it is that makes you come alive, vibrating with intensity, feeling and passion, you, too, will have found your bliss.

A voracious reader, I love to play with words on the written page.

---

[64] Greer, Steven. (2006). *Hidden Truth - Forbidden Knowledge* (p 270). Crozet, VA: Crossing Point, Inc.

A lover of history, I lose all track of time when engaged in research directly related to my own personal genealogies.

A disseminator of information, I attempt to share truth as per my Portals of Spirit [65] website.

Alternative healing modalities (crystals, meditation, orgonite devices, healing layouts, Reiki) have become my way of giving back to myself and others, including Mother Gaia.

These are what currently constitute *my* bliss.

As has long been known, a few manipulate while billions allow themselves to be manipulated. The pertinent question to be asking in this situation is … where does the real responsibility lie?

We cannot be controlled unless we allow ourselves to be.

The reality is that we are all One.

Everyone else's freedom, then, becomes our own.

---

[65] http://www.portalsofspirit.com

When we "get ourselves right, the world must come right because we are the world and the world is us. Society is the sum total of human thinking and feeling. It is a reflection of our attitudes. When we change them, we change society. We are only a change of mind away from real freedom, the freedom to express our God-given uniqueness and celebrate the diversity of gifts, perceptions and inspiration that exist within the collective human psyche." [66]

In keeping with an online article, entitled *Living With The Matrix or The Irreversible Effect of Developing Blue Pill Resistance ...*

One of the key scenes in "The Matrix" is when Neo, played by Keanu Reeves, has to choose between the blue and the red pill. Once he has taken the red pill, he no longer is fooled by the imaginary world the Matrix has created for its captives. He suddenly can recognize the Matrix for what it is and how it operates. While the Matrix in the movie is a machine that has trapped

---

[66] Icke, David. (1999). *The Biggest Secret* (p 493). Scottsdale, AZ: Bridge of Love Publications USA.

mankind in cocoons as a source of electrical energy, the Matrix in the real world has trapped us as a source of income in a world of taxes, interest rates, and consumerism.

I can't decide which Matrix is worse, the one in the movie, or the one in the outside world. For generations now, we have been fooled into believing that we live in a world of freedom and human rights, where we elect our governments and are protected by the rule of law. We are told that in return for that privilege we have to pay tax, rent and interest, and, at times, go to war to protect this wonderful way of life.

While the simpler minds amongst us are kept quiet with a modern version of ancient Rome's bread and games, the more educated people are filled with gigabytes of illusionary data, tricking them into believing they live in a world that only exists in their heads, [meaning] **an enlightened society, where everything is so much better than in the Dark Ages of the past,** [where all are] **a big family, a caring society that ensures that everybody is taken care of and nobody discriminated against.**

What worries me the most is how the ruling elite in recent years has decided that it no longer needs to be so 'caring'. It got cocky and felt that 'wasting' so much money on maintaining the illusion is no longer required. The big project of creating the New World Order is almost complete and the mind-control so powerful, our self chosen rulers, have decided that they can risk cutting down on welfare, public health and education, and all those other spoils that kept the masses happy after the debacle of World War II.

Like in the movie, where taking the red pill suddenly allowed Neo to see through the Matrix, doing so in the real world has an irreversible effect. Once we realize that the world we live in is nothing but an illusion, the rest is just a matter of time.

The real world, the world of the Matrix, is right in front of our eyes. The same data [be we blue pillers or red pillers] means totally different things, and once we have

seen the face of the evil machine, there is no turning back. [67]

As Jean-Claude Koven had previously stated, **I am a member of the Truth of the Moment club. Just don't hold me to it tomorrow. Whatever this archive said, just remember that it occurred on this particular day in this particular year. And that is what I thought I saw then. Tomorrow, I think I'll see something else.**

Therein lies the beauty of growth, the beauty of change.

All I can say, right here, right now, is that this is what I see.

I am very much a believer in the strength and tenacity of the human spirit.

We can change things, beginning with our very selves. In changing one's self, you are able to affect change on others.

---

[67] http://100777.com/matrix4

I believe in complete and total disengagement from the Matrix as this is the way to regaining what we have lost, what we have given away, what is rightfully ours, what has always been ours, and what we *must* take the time to reclaim.

In the illuminating words of Andrew Cohen, editor of EnlightenNext Magazine … *When we stop being a seeker and become a finder, we no longer have any doubt about who we really are and why we are here on Earth. In our own direct awakening to Spirit's true face, existential doubt dies a sudden and irrevocable death, liberating an infectious confidence that is rooted deep within our souls.*

A true finder may or may not continue to engage in spiritual practice, but if he or she does, it is motivated only by the desire to continue *to evolve for the sake of the evolutionary process itself.*

Indeed, in evolutionary spirituality, making the noble effort to catalyze our own individual and collective higher development is recognized to be the very raison d'être *of human beings at the leading edge.*

And we can only begin to do this when we have given up seeking forever.

Then and only then will we stop reaching for a spiritual epiphany to convince us of something.

We instead make the effort to evolve because we are in love with life and are committed to unlocking its highest potentials through our own development. Those potentials will only come to the fore when we are no longer trying to become *enlightened but have let go of any other option than to be the expression of the highest we have seen and experienced, in all our imperfection, right now.*

That's what it means to be a finder.

Addendum

Officially begun on March 26, 2008, everything written previous to this point was written when I was still basking in the full moon energies of the March 21 spring equinox (as a participant in the world-wide Solar Wave 2008 event) and released as an ebook in April 2008.

There have been countless other books, coupled with online research, all of which has been absorbed these last three years; too many, in fact, to mention here. What follow now simply represents the culmination of my current truths.

Always a researcher, always a seeker, what struck me the most was the fact that we create our own reality.

What this initially means is that you can either continue to see yourself as a defeated victim or you can begin to see yourself as an empowered, powerful and cognizant creator.

That becomes the first monumental decision to be made.

Developing feelings of self-worth are also crucial to the overall process. Unless you learn to love yourself, to forgive yourself and to accept who you are (meaning all aspects of yourself), you are not going to be able to make the advances that you want to make.

Every conceivable life possibility already exists.

You simply have to decide what it is that you want.

You can manipulate your reality by changing your thoughts, words and actions. This is something that takes dedication and discipline on a daily basis until you reach the point whereby the exertion becomes automatic and effortless.

You *are* creating the world around you.

Reality is not something that is happening to you. As an observer, it is you who is creating your reality.

Your world, quite simply, is what you make it out to be.

As long as you remain focused on anger, revenge, hatred (and any other negative based emotion), you are going to continue to attract more of the very same into your life.

By comparison, when you are happy and content, you will find yourself surrounded by jubilant and fulfilled circumstances (individuals, places, events).

In wanting to live a more positive life, you must be willing to make some immediate changes.

You must take the time to avoid negative people and negative situations (events). Stop watching the news. Do your best to stop listening to the constant chatter in your head, taking the time, instead, to focus on your breathing in an effort to reach that place of stillness that exists within.

As you learn to surrender your conscious ego to your subconscious mind, that true part of you that knows your passions, you will come to understand that everything in your life, be it good or bad, is being created by you at a higher level.

This shall become the moment that you will endeavor to create by design (creation at a conscious level) as opposed to continuing to create by default (creation at an unconscious level).

As well, this becomes the moment when you realize that you must take complete ownership and responsibility for all that you have been creating; a most empowering time to behold.

When you embrace your purpose … to discover who you are, to become increasingly self-aware, to grow by keeping an open mind, to change your opinions, to discover your truths (which are always changing), to learn through experience, to be sure of the present moment, to respect the choices that you make for yourself, to respect the choices that others make for themselves (without judgment), to awaken to the realization that you are your mind, to awaken to the realization that you are God … as well as your passion, you will become united with Source; your true divine self.

I leave you with these steadfast rules to life and living.

[1] Listen to yourself (intuition, feelings, nudges).

[2] Follow your heart (dreams).

[3] Be good to yourself.

[4] Do unto others as you would have them do unto you.

[5] Give of the heart (compassion, kindness, respect, love, compliments, tolerance).

[6] Take responsibility and own your life.

[7] Maintain a positive and uplifting state of mind.

[8] Focus on happiness and contentment (following your bliss).

[9] Continue to remain open minded to new ideas (thinking outside the box).

[10] Allow your mind to lead you to oneness.

As you recognize synchronicity in your life, you may rest assured in the knowing that you are on the right path.

When you are able to master the communication process between your conscious mind (ego) and your subconscious mind (higher self), through both positive dictates and the surrendering of your ego, in that it merges with the mandates of the heart, you will have become a master of your universe.

If I may leave you with yet another quote from Andrew Cohen, editor of EnlightenNext Magazine … *In spiritual evolution, there are no guarantees. Life is unpredictable. So this path requires both an unconditional commitment to victory and enormous patience.*

If we are very serious about this endeavor, we have to become the exemplars ourselves. It has to start with our own unconditional commitment to victory, knowing that there are no guarantees. The very fact that there are no guarantees underlines how urgent our commitment is, because we don't know how much time we each have to do this. We don't know how long we're going to be here. So the worst thing we can do is to waste time.

Traditional enlightenment is about going beyond time, but Evolutionary enlightenment is about doing something in *time, because evolution can only happen in time. Therefore,* don't waste time.

From the perspective of evolution, time is the most precious commodity. Time is all we have to develop.

Many of us have been culturally trained to spend an enormous amount of time worrying about our psychological needs and desires, our ego's fears and concerns. And this is understandable, but the problem is that it robs us of time that could be used to participate in life in a much deeper way.

If you have the strength and clarity to look at your own life from this perspective, you won't want to allow yourself to waste time, because you will realize you are wasting the precious chance you actually have to evolve.

Thank you for sharing your time with me.

About the Author

Michele Doucette is webmistress of Portals of Spirit, a spirituality website whereby one will find links to [1] The Enlightened Scribe, [2] an ezine called Gateway To The Soul, [3] books of spiritual resonance as well as authors of metaphysical importance, [4] categories of interest from Angels to Zen, [5] up-to-date information as shared by a Quantum Healer, [6] affiliate programs and resources of personal significance, [7] healing resource advertisements and [8] spiritual news.

As a Level 2 Reiki Practitioner, she sends long distance Reiki to those who make the request, claiming only to be a facilitator of the Universal energy, meaning that it is up to the individual(s) in question to use these energies in order to heal themselves.

Having also acquired a Crystal Healing Practitioner diploma (Stonebridge College in the UK), she is guardian to many from the mineral kingdom.

She is the author of several spiritual/metaphysical works; namely, [1] *The Ultimate Enlightenment For 2012: All We Need Is Ourselves*, [2] *Turn Off The TV: Turn On Your Mind*, [3] *Veracity At Its Best*, [4] *The Collective: Essays on Reality* (a composition of essays in relation to the Matrix), [5] *Sleepers Awaken: The Time Is Now To Consciously Create Your Own Reality*, [6] *Healing the Planet and Ourselves: How To Raise Your Vibration*, [7] *You Are Everything: Everything Is You* and [8] *The Awakening of Humanity: A Foremost Necessity*, all of which have been published through St. Clair Publications.

In addition, she has written a separate volume that deals with crystals, aptly entitled *The Wisdom of Crystals*.

She is also the author of *A Travel in Time to Grand Pré*, a visionary metaphysical novel that historically ties the descendants of Yeshua (Jesus) to modern day Nova Scotia.

As shared by a reviewer, it is *Veracity At Its Best*, a spiritual (metaphysical) tome, that "constructs the context for the spiritual message" imparted in *A Travel in Time to Grand Pré*.

Against the backdrop of 1754 Acadie, it was the blending of French Acadian history with current DNA testing that contributed to the weaving of this alchemical tale of time travel, romance and intrigue.

From Henry I Sinclair to the Merovingians, from the Cathari treasure at Montségur to the Knights Templar, this novel, together with the words of Yeshua as spoken at the height of his ministry, has the potential to inspire others; for it is herein that we learn how individuals can find their way, their truth(s), so as to live their lives to the fullest.

www.ingramcontent.com/pod-product-compliance
Lightning Source LLC
LaVergne TN
LVHW010105110826
845155LV00028B/496

* 9 7 8 1 9 3 5 7 8 6 2 1 4 *